KIDDING AROUND

Washington, D.C.

A YOUNG PERSON'S GUIDE TO THE CITY

ANNE PEDERSEN

ILLUSTRATED BY JIM FINNELL

John Muir Publications
Santa Fe, New Mexico

This book is affectionately dedicated to Mark and Claire Pedersen, my energetic research assistants and fledgling quality control experts.

John Muir Publications, P.O. Box 613, Santa Fe, NM 87504

First edition. Third printing

Library of Congress Cataloging-in-Publication Data
Pedersen, Anne, 1949-
    Kidding around Washington, D.C.

    Summary: A guidebook to Washington, D.C., surveying such areas as Capitol Hill, the Mall museums, monuments, parks, Georgetown, and nearby Virginia.
    1. Washington (D.C.)—Description—1981-   —Guidebooks—Juvenile literature.   2. Children—Travel—Washington (D.C.)—Guide books—Juvenile Literature.
    Washington (D.C.)—Description—[Guides]   1. Title
F192.3P43   1989   917.53'044   88-43530
ISBN 0-945465-25-4

Typeface: Trump Medieval
Typesetter: Copygraphics, Santa Fe, New Mexico
Designer: Joanna V. Hill
Printer: Guynes Printing Company of New Mexico, Inc.

Distributed to the book trade by:
W. W. Norton & Company, Inc.
New York, New York

Contents

1. Why Do People Visit Washington?

Washington is located on the east coast of the United States, about midway between Maine and Georgia. The city is situated where two rivers, the Potomac and the Anacostia, come together. The land is mostly flat, and for years a lot of what is now downtown Washington was marshland.

The most obvious reason is that it's the nation's capital. Washington is where the president lives; where Congress meets and drafts the laws of our land; where the Supreme Court decides questions about the interpretation of these laws. If you think of the United States as a living body, Washington is the heart. It's an exciting feeling to be so close to the center of things: that helicopter hovering over the White House lawn could have the president in it; that man or woman sitting next to you on the Senate subway could be a politician you've seen many times on the news. The actual workings of government are hard to see, but nowhere else in the world can you get as close to them as you can in Washington.

Washington is often called "America's hometown." From the Apollo moon landing module in the Air and Space Museum to John Dillinger's death mask at the FBI, the city is full of things that belong to each and every American. Some of them, like the death mask, may not be among the things you expect. But remember, they are yours.

Wait, there's more. Washington is not all government and history. It's a big international city, which means you can find almost anything you want here.

A trip to Washington can be a real adventure. This book is designed to make it even more of one. It tells you about things you can enjoy doing and seeing—you, not necessarily your parents. Everything suggested in this book may not interest you. People are different: some like spacecraft and others like dolls' houses. So pick and choose.

Oh, one more thing. Most of the stuff people tell you to see in Washington is really worth seeing. It may not seem very original to take a tour of the Capitol or visit the Lincoln Memorial, but the feeling you will get when you gaze at the statue of Freedom on that great white dome or stand at Lincoln's feet is not one that can be duplicated anywhere else. So go ahead—be a tourist! See new places, have new experiences. This is what traveling is all about.

The District of Columbia is only 69 square miles in area. Washington is a city (named after George Washington) inside a federal district ("D" for district, "C" for Christopher Columbus), so it's really a city without a state.

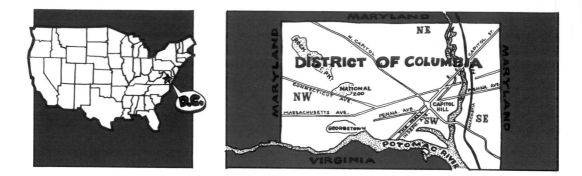

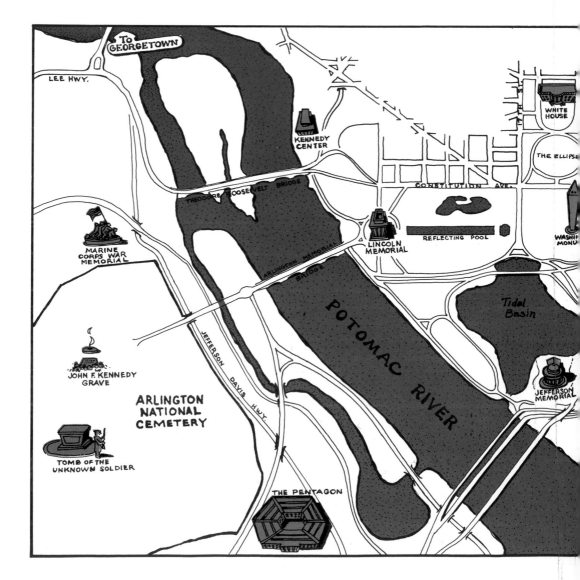

2. Where It Is

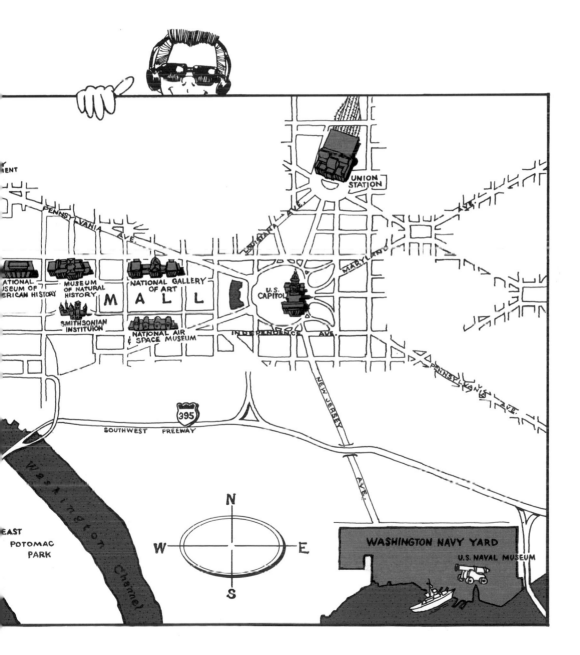

3. The Early Years of the Capital City

nlike most cities, which spring into existence because people spontaneously decide to settle there, Washington is a planned city. After the War of Independence there was much debate between the northern and southern states over where to put the permanent home of the new national government. Finally, two of the political leaders of the day, New Yorker Alexander Hamilton and Virginian Thomas Jefferson, worked out a deal. The northern states had accumulated more debt during the revolution than the southern states. The South agreed to support a proposal that the federal government pay all war debts, if, in turn, the North backed a plan to build the new capital city on the banks of the Potomac River near the thriving ports of Georgetown and Alexandria.

George Washington chose the exact site of the new capital. He also chose French engineer Pierre L'Enfant to design the city. L'Enfant came up with a plan that was considered radical for its day—a gridlike design with broad streets and diagonal avenues, public buildings on high points of land, and many parks and circles. Because he did not get along with many of the

people he had to work with, L'Enfant was dismissed from his post in 1792, only a year after he was appointed. However, his basic design is the blueprint for the city we see today.

Work on the White House (then called the President's House) began in 1792, and construction of the Capitol a year later. In 1800, with both buildings unfinished, the government moved from Philadelphia to Washington, which had just 3,000 residents and barely enough buildings to house them. The only business in existence was a brewery, and what is now the Mall was a swamp. People were not eager to buy land in the new capital, even at less than $100 a lot (today a lot costs hundreds of thousands of dollars!) for Washington was a rough, uncomfortable place to live. As if the new city didn't have enough problems, in 1812 the United States went to war with Great Britain again, and in

When Washington was founded, there was concern that local politics might interfere with the workings of the federal government. So residents of the city were not allowed to vote in congressional or presidential elections. Today, they are able to vote for president, but the District still has no real representation in Congress. There is a delegate in the House of Representatives, but he or she can only vote in committee, not in regular sessions of Congress.

1814 British forces marched into the capital and burned the Capitol, the White House, and other public buildings almost to the ground. Construction had to start all over again.

During the Civil War, Washington resembled a giant Union camp. Troops were quartered everywhere, even in the Capitol and the White House. Alexandria, just across the Potomac, flew the Confederate flag, and in 1864 Confederate forces penetrated to the edge of the city. After the war, thousands of freed slaves made their way to the nation's capital to join the many people who were there to help in the war effort.

Washington was no longer a small town, but it still lacked many things a city should have: sidewalks, street lights, water and gas mains, a decent police force. In the 1870s a city administrator named Alexander "Boss" Shepherd took care of a lot of these needs. In the process he spent four times as much money as the city had given him for the job. He bankrupted Washington, but the improvements he created made it a more pleasant and safer place.

The twentieth century has brought with it two world wars and an ever-increasing federal bureaucracy, all of which have furthered the transformation of Washington into the handsome, busy place it is today. The city you see, with its many large buildings and leafy parks, is a far cry from the muddy little town called by one nineteeth-century observer a collection of "small, miserable huts."

4. The Feel of the City

There are about 636,000 people living in the District. The greater Washington area (the city plus suburbs) has a population of about 3.5 million.

When you arrive, you'll see that Washington is a pretty city. Everywhere you look green parks beckon and fountains gurgle. It's an international city, too. You'll hear foreign languages and see people in different national dress. Many live and work here, while others, like you, have come to visit.

The architecture is varied. Brick and stone rowhouses in Georgetown have a cozy feel. Modern office buildings stand next to ornate Victorian mansions. The buildings are not tall. In fact, there are few taller than 130 feet, so the Capitol and the monuments can be seen easily from far away. But the fact that the buildings aren't high doesn't mean they aren't big. There are some near the Mall and downtown that cover several city blocks.

If after strolling past a few of these massive structures, you feel you need a more people-sized experience, you can visit a few of the street vendors nearby. They're all over, selling all sorts of souvenirs and snacks. You can buy as many T-shirts as you could possibly want, have a Coke and some popcorn, and even try on some reasonably good jewelry. On a more political

Metro stations are all the same, big tunnels with roofs and walls like a curved waffle; it's worth a subway ride just to see them.

note, you can have your picture taken with a life-sized cutout of the president on many street corners, or, in an election year, the candidate of your choice.

You want to get across town? No problem. It is easy to get around Washington. The city is divided into four sections: Northeast, Northwest, Southeast, and Southwest, with the Capitol at the center of things. Most of what you will want to see is in the Northwest area, the largest of the four sections. Streets form a grid pattern (remember L'Enfant?) with lettered streets running east to west and numbered streets north to south. Avenues crisscross the grid, radiating out from parks and circles like spokes from a wheel.

One of the best ways to get around downtown is to walk. Bring comfortable shoes with you so your feet won't ache from traipsing around. If you do get tired, and you're on the Mall, you can hop on a Tourmobile. These red, white, and blue buses come complete with tour guides. They stop at 18 places on and near the Mall and in Arlington. You can buy an all-day pass and get on and off when and where you wish.

The public buses in Washington will take you almost anywhere, but they can be confusing. The subway, however, is fast, clean, safe, and easy to use. There are four intersecting color-coded Metro lines, and transferring from one to another is simple. Except during rush hour, there are also lots of taxis around. They charge by a zone system: your fare is determined by how many zones you cross rather than by a meter.

Winters in Washington generally are not too bad, but summers are often hot and humid. Spring and fall are the best times to visit, but

Nineteen million people visit Washington every year, and most of them come when the weather is hot. Ask your parents to find a hotel with a swimming pool: it makes all the difference at the end of a steamy day of sightseeing.

they're also when you go to school, so chances are you'll be seeing the city in the summer. If so, be prepared for some long lines.

One more thing: don't forget to check the local papers during your stay to find out about special things going on that you might be interested in. A section in the *Washington Post* Weekend/Friday magazine, "Saturday's Child," has a calendar of events for the week. Other publications have listings as well.

5. Capitol Hill

amed for the Capitol Building that dominates it, the "hill" is Jenkins Hill, one of the highest points of land in the District. L'Enfant located the Capitol here so it could be seen from all over the city. If you poke around behind the Capitol, away from the Mall and the public buildings, you'll find a pretty residential neighborhood where many professional people live.

The Capitol
A definite must-see. Floodlit by night, white and gleaming by day, the huge building with the great dome is the literal center of the city.

The official tour (which is short and worth taking) starts in the Rotunda, directly underneath the dome. This room is awesome in size and scope. Look up. One hundred eighty feet above you on the curved ceiling is a magnificent fresco, *The Apotheosis of Washington*, painted by an Italian immigrant named Constantino Brumidi who lay flat on his back on a scaffold for eleven months to finish it (some of the figures are 15 feet high). Circling the room are statues and paintings of scenes from early American history. In the center of the floor is a simple white

The Capitol dome is the second the building has had (the first was much smaller). It is made of iron and weighs 9 million pounds. You can't tell, but tests have shown that it moves very slightly in high winds and expands or contracts as much as four inches on very hot or cold days.

The statue on top of the dome is of a woman, Freedom. She is 19.5 feet high and weighs 7.5 tons. Some people think she looks like an American Indian.

Confused about the difference between capi**tal** and capi**tol**? A capital city is one where the national or state government has offices and meetings. The Capitol is the building where legislative sessions are held.

If the Senate is in session, a flag flies over the north end of the Capitol, where the Senate Chamber is. If the House is in session, there is a flag over the southern end. If either the House or Senate is in night session, a light burns on the upper dome.

During the Civil War, 3,000 soldiers slept in the Capitol building. There was a mess kitchen and a bakery in the basement.

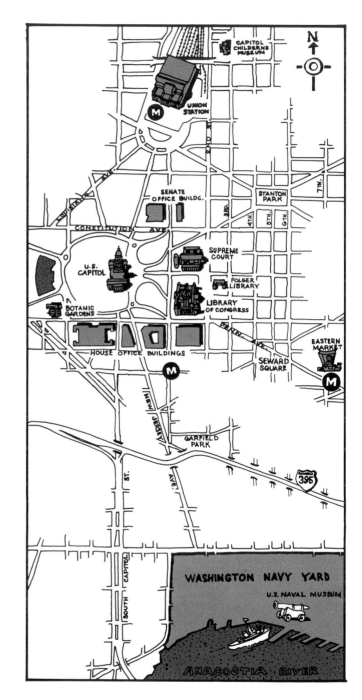

stone where 25 Americans (including 7 presidents), the first of them Abraham Lincoln, have lain in state before burial.

Next to the Rotunda is Statuary Hall. This room was the House of Representatives chamber from 1807 to 1857. It's known as the "Whispering Room" because you can clearly hear a person whisper from far on the other side of the chamber. The room is now ringed with statues given to the government by various states—hence its name.

The tour continues downstairs to the "Crypt" directly underneath the Rotunda, where it ends. But you should keep going. You haven't seen half of the interesting stuff there is to see.

Explore the corridors. You'll see doors with signs on them like "Speaker of the House"; you'll also come across the Old Senate Chamber and the Old Supreme Court Chamber, which will give you a sense of how much smaller government used to be.

To see the present Senate or House in session you have to get a pass from the office of your senator or congressman (no big deal—it takes about 15 minutes). Catch the private subway to the Senate or House office buildings. These nifty little underground trolleys leave every few minutes, and there's usually a lot of activity in the stations. Pages and congressional staffers hurry to and fro with a great sense of purpose, while bells sound periodically to signal what's going on upstairs. There's excitement in the air, and it's catching. The congressional office buildings look pretty much like any others, but here, too, you get that "corridors of power" feeling. The names on the office doors are probably ones you

Other Things to Do at the Capitol:
Feed the squirrels on the west lawn. There are lots of them, so if you have any peanuts left over from your plane trip bring them along and make some friends.

Take a drink from the fountain in the grotto at the foot of the hill on the northwest side of the lawn (near Constitution Ave.). This secluded brick alcove with bubbling fountain is easy to miss, but it's a good place to sit down, relax, and plan your next move.

Be sure and take in the view of the city from the West Front (this is where the president gets inaugurated, unless it's too cold). You can see all the way past the Washington Monument and Lincoln Memorial across the river to Arlington.

know from reading the paper or watching TV. If you're lucky you'll get a glimpse of your senator or congressman when you pick up your pass. If you're really enterprising, write to him or her before your trip and ask if you can make an appointment to say hello. If they're not too busy, members of Congress are usually happy to see their constituents.

Another place you are likely to see famous people is on the floor of the House or Senate chamber. But don't be disappointed if all you see is a handful of sleepy-looking congressmen, a page or two, and someone making a speech about an issue you've never heard of. As a rule, government is not much of a spectator sport.

Supreme Court

Across the east lawn of the Capitol, on the side away from the Mall, is the Supreme Court. This building, which looks like a Greek temple even though it was built in 1935, is home to the highest court in the country. The Supreme Court is made up of nine justices, or judges, who decide whether laws are constitutional or not; it also reviews cases sent to it from lower courts when the issues in those cases merit special attention or affect the lives of many Americans.

If the court is sitting, and you're interested in law, a visit to the courtroom may be in order. The judges wear black robes and sit in front of a red velvet curtain while they hear cases; there are a lot of theatrical touches to the way business is conducted. You may not want to stay for arguments, but then again you may: if you do, be prepared to listen hard and follow complex discussions.

Union Station

This imposing marble building, built in 1907, has just been renovated. After years of being used for other purposes, it is now a train station again, as well as a very classy indoor mall with restaurants, movie theaters, and some great shops. Check out the train store, which stocks virtually everything you can think of that has to do with railroads.

Capitol Children's Museum

This museum is close behind Union Station. Once inside the outer gate (the museum is a building inside a complex of other buildings), you are welcomed by a fantastic array of glittering figures created out of everyday objects and trash by an Indian artist. In the museum itself, you can run an old-fashioned hand printing press, track a satellite on a computer, watch a cartoon, or get lost in a funhouse maze. If you're tired of looking at things and want to *do* for a change, this place is for you.

Washington Navy Yard and Museum

A little off the beaten track, but well worth the visit, is the Navy Yard on the Anacostia River. There is a museum in an old hangar full of antique and new weapons, dioramas of battles, planes, scale models of ships of all sorts, bombs (including replicas of the first atomic bombs), and more. There are even antiaircraft guns (unloaded, of course) that you can climb up on and aim.

Outside, in a little park by the river, is a small arsenal of naval artifacts from the last 100 years. Cheek by jowl are German naval guns, missiles, cannons, and anchors 7 feet high. Right next door in the river lies a retired destroyer, the *Barry*, which you can explore from top to bottom. Check out the bunks, the kitchen, the bridge, and combat center. Then imagine spending six months at sea on this boat with 330 other people, and you begin to get an idea of what active naval duty is like.

Other Things to See in the Capitol Hill Area
Right behind the Capitol, on the southeast side, stands the original **Library of Congress** building, which resembles a Victorian birthday cake. There are now three buildings housing the Library's vast collection of books, photographs, and prints, but this one is the oldest. On display on the main floor is one of three existing perfect copies of the Gutenberg Bible, the first book ever printed using movable metal type. There's a tour (almost every public building in Washington seems to have a tour), and the main reading room is worth seeing for its size and high domed ceiling.

Next to the Library of Congress is the **Folger Library**, which serves as a research center for Renaissance and Shakespearean scholars. Inside is a working theater that is a replica of a theater from Shakespeare's time.

A favorite here is the underwater pressure sphere from the bathyscaphe Alvin, *which looks like a mammoth hand grenade.*

There is a funny-looking building at the bottom of the southeast lawn of the Capitol (Mall side) with a roof that looks like a bunch of glass onions. This is the **U.S. Botanic Garden**, basically a big steamy greenhouse filled with every kind of plant and flower you can think of. It is a good place to rest your feet and pretend you're in the tropics.

If you are in the Capitol Hill area on a Saturday, take a hike down Pennsylvania Avenue a few blocks east of the Capitol to **Eastern Market**. This colorful outdoor bazaar and farmers' market has all kinds of vendors selling all kinds of things. There's also an indoor market where you can sit and eat. It's crowded, noisy, and fun—a good place to get a feel for nontourist Washington, as local families shop here regularly.

6. The Mall Museums

ike a wide green carpet, the National Mall extends for two miles from the Capitol past the Washington Monument to the Lincoln Memorial. The end near the Capitol is flanked by the many museums of the Smithsonian Institution. Even if you don't usually like museums, you'll like these. You could easily spend several days, even weeks, marveling at all the treasures in these wonderful places.

Note: Most of these museums have tours, but you may have more fun if you poke around by yourself on your own schedule. Most also have places to eat.

National Air and Space Museum
An absolute, positive must-see. This could be the most fascinating place in all of Washington. Opened in 1976, it is crammed with every conceivable kind of satellite, plane, and spacecraft, from the Wright brothers' original 1903 "flying machine" to a duplicate of the Apollo moon landing module.

There are three two-story halls, one at each end of the building and one in the middle. Wander through these first. Above you float satellites

*For those of you who just can't get enough of things that fly, the Smithsonian has another air and space museum in Suitland, Maryland. The **Paul E. Garber Facility** has mostly planes but also a few space items. It is primarily for storage and restoration, but there are tours available if you call ahead and a big open house one weekend in the spring.*

In the late nineteenth century, railroad tracks covered much of what is now the Mall between the Capitol and the Washington Monument.

and space probes, some looking like exotic foil-and-net insects; they seem awfully fragile to have traveled so far. The ceilings are crowded with aircraft; huge rockets and missiles jut up from the floor. Part of the Skylab orbital workshop sits like a huge silver barrel in the Space Hall (you can walk through it). The many smaller galleries, though less spectacular, are no less interesting. There are exhibits on planets, ballooning, the history of flight, and more.

Be sure to take in a film at the Langley Auditorium (ground floor), even if there's a line (this museum is usually crowded). The screen is the height of a five-story building and the large-format projection system makes you feel as though you're actually *in* the picture. Your stomach jumps as you zoom off the top of a cliff, or land on a dime on an aircraft carrier. If you are a space buff, you'll want to see "The Dream Is Alive," about our space program. It features spectacular footage shot in space and, poignantly, some sequences of astronauts who died in the *Challenger* tragedy in 1986.

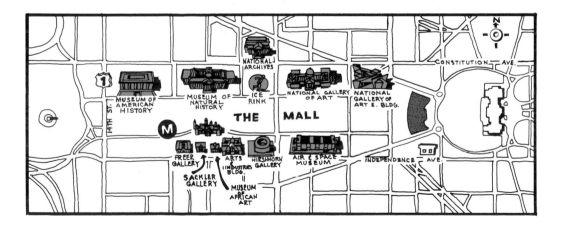

Also, don't miss the planetarium on the second floor. Its program "State of the Universe" takes you on a vivid trip to our solar system and beyond. And don't forget the gift shop on the first floor, which offers model kites, books on aviation and space, unusual toys, and, yes, T-shirts.

Check out the short film, Powers of Ten, in the Star Hall, and travel from light-years out in the universe to the center of a single atom.

National Gallery

Across the Mall from the Air and Space Museum, the National Gallery comes in two parts: the West Building (the big old one) and the East Building (the sharp-edged trapezoid with the abstract sculptures around it).

Just outside the front door of the East Building, often called the I. M. Pei building after the architect who designed it, is a fifteen-foot, dull

What you might like: the Impressionist paintings ('19th C. on the map). When you see them you'll understand why people visit museums instead of just looking at pictures in books. The colors and details here are far more vivid and alive than any reproduction could possibly be. Also check out the Renaissance collection, just across the rotunda.

bronze, two-piece sculpture by the British artist Henry Moore (you can play hide-and-seek between the slabs). This is art you may want to touch, and you can. Feel how cool and smooth the surfaces are. Inside, the building soars upward to a glass ceiling. Above you like a bird hangs a huge red, blue, and black Calder mobile, graceful and light-seeming in spite of its size.

The multilevel building invites you to explore. Upstairs and down are galleries that offer modern art at its best: color, movement, drama, humor. These pictures work on the senses; they invite participation. There's a room full of intense, brooding Rothkos, and another is devoted to Barnett Newman's spare, black and white *Stations of the Cross*. Sit in these rooms for a while and see how you feel. Then check out Andy Warhol's soup cans. Who says art has to be serious?

Most of what you will want to see in the West Building is on the main floor. The layout can be confusing; by all means, pick up a free map at the information booth near the central rotunda. It can also be overwhelming. Room follows room in a bewildering richness, and if you're not careful, sensory overload may follow close behind. The paintings here are very different from those in the East Building. Most are much older. But they reflect the times in which they were painted in much the same way that the modern art in the East Building reflects the pace and culture of today. Many are religious in theme; others are huge canvases with all sorts of things going on in them. Some, frankly, you may find boring and hard to relate to. If this happens, move on. The National Gallery is so big, and has so many different types of art in it, that you're bound to find something that moves or pleases you.

Some tips for viewing, here and in other museums: Pace yourself. Don't try to look at too much at once. Look at a few things and study them well. Try to figure out what the artist wanted to say; sometimes the clues are in the details. Some paintings clearly tell a story. Others are portraits or show religious scenes. Maybe the artist is inviting the viewer to see familiar things differently—how does he or she accomplish this? Usually the more you look at art, the more you notice.

You can get from the East Building to the West in two ways: either walk past the fountain outside or take the moving walkway in the underground tunnel. This way you get to see the glassed-in waterfall that's the underside of the fountain.

If you're tired, have a seat in the rotunda or one of the garden courts. Their fountains and greenery are very relaxing.

National Museum of Natural History

The first thing you see in the front rotunda is a huge African bush elephant (stuffed), his trunk raised as if to trumpet hello. His welcome is appropriate, for this is a user-friendly museum. Its resources are awesome: millions of items from the natural world as well as all sorts of artifacts from different cultures around the globe. But the museum itself does not overwhelm you with information. It is all there but clearly organized and imaginatively laid out. You can see as much or as little as you like.

Visit the **Dinosaur Hall**, chock-full of triceratops, diplodicus, stegosaurus, camptosaurus, and other prehistoric goodies. Nearby, the fossil mammal hall has mastodon and giant sloth skeletons—very satisfying.

Speaking of bones, there's an entire hall devoted to nothing but, with skeletons of everything from rats to whales. You'll find it on the way to the **Insect Zoo**. Ever seen a scorpion the size of a small crab? A tarantula eat a banana? The Insect Zoo has these and more. It's a whole room filled with bugs of every conceivable kind—caged, of course, although there are times when some are let out under supervision. Don't miss it.

The **Gem and Mineral Halls** upstairs are where you'll find huge crystals, topaz big as hens' eggs, and, sitting behind *very* thick glass, the Hope Diamond, at 45.5 carats the biggest blue diamond in the world. Also upstairs: moon rocks and meteorites. Downstairs, the **Sea Hall** boasts a life-sized model of a blue whale suspended from the ceiling as well as models of the *Alvin* and *Hydrolab*, underwater research vehicles. Also worth investigating is the **Discovery Room**,

a "hands-on" lab where you can handle shells, bones, and other natural artifacts. All through the museum are incredibly realistic dioramas, three-dimensional scenes of animal and cultural life against a painted background. Some of the best are in the **Mammal Hall**.

National Museum of American History
The Smithsonian Institution has often been dubbed "America's attic" because of its vast collection of all things American. If the name fits, then the Museum of American History in particular must be America's attic, basement, and storage shed combined. It's a fascinating hodgepodge of everything from the original Star Spangled Banner (on display in the second floor lobby) to old radios, light bulbs, and the inaugural gowns of First Ladies. There is so much here it can be confusing, and it is easy to get lost. Pick up a map, but don't count on it to explain everything. A lot of the halls have low light levels and many of the exhibits are noisy: video terminals talk, machinery buzzes, music plays. You really have to concentrate on what you are looking at.

What to see? The Foucault Pendulum, a huge brass bob suspended from a steel cable, demonstrates the rotation of the earth in the Mall lobby. The electricity and telephone exhibits house a dizzying collection of machinery: you can place a call from one phone to another next to it and see the mechanics of how the call is transmitted in the panel frame (whirr, click). Other things to inspect: old locomotives, tractors, sewing machines, coins. The "Nation of Nations" exhibit reveals, among other things, how an Italian-American family would have lived in 1940. Compare their simple rooms to those in your own house, and think about what a difference fifty years have made.

When you are tired, skip down to the first floor and have a sundae or sandwich in the nineteenth-century ice-cream parlor. And definitely visit the gift shop. It is the biggest and best among the Smithsonian shops, with crafts, jewelry, books, and a huge toy section.

Smithsonian Castle/Freer Gallery of Art/ National Museum of African Art/Arthur M. Sackler Gallery

Across the Mall from the Museum of American History rises a peculiar red sandstone building with turrets and towers. It is the Smithsonian "Castle." This building is headquarters to all of the Institution's museums.

Behind the Castle are three other museums. The Freer Gallery of Art, which specializes in Asian and Near Eastern art, will be closed for renovation until 1991. However, if you want to see some beautiful Buddhas and jade, visit the Arthur M. Sackler Gallery, one of two new underground museums recently built beneath the lovely garden in back of the Castle. Its companion, the National Museum of African Art, is equally fine and has great scary masks.

Arts and Industries Building
Next to the Castle is the Victorian brick Arts and Industries Building, which houses objects from the Centennial Exhibition of 1876. Stroll through and admire the steam engine, boat models, and Baldwin locomotive. Here also you can find the **Discovery Theatre**, which presents musical and dramatic performances for children October through June.

The Castle will be closed to visitors through late 1989 for remodeling. In the spring and summer months, however, an old-fashioned carousel operates out front: $1.00 for the horse of your choice.

The Smithsonian, which is thought of as the most American of museums, was started by an Englishman, James Smithson. He left his fortune to this country with instructions to found the institution that bears his name.

Even though these museums are underground, they're easy to spot. Each has a gray granite pavilion at ground level with similar roofs: one covered with little domes, the other with pyramids.

Hirshhorn Museum and Sculpture Garden

The Hirshhorn is that big gray concrete "doughnut" sitting between the Arts and Industries Building and the Air and Space Museum. Opened in 1974, its collection reflects the newest of the new in modern art. Have at it if you want to increase your artistic vocabulary—you'll be stimulated, moved, confused, and possibly even annoyed. If not, take a stroll through the sunken sculpture garden and see how varied sculpture can be.

Near the Mall

Set back across Constitution Avenue is the **National Archives** (like the Supreme Court, it, too, resembles a temple), home to the originals of the Declaration of Independence, the Bill of Rights, and the Constitution. You can see these documents, protected by special cases and an elaborate alarm system, if you go inside.

There's an outdoor ice rink on the Mall side of the Archives, so if you visit Washington in the winter you can go skating there.

7. Monuments, Parks, and Money

To most people, Washington means monuments. The city is full of them, but the most famous, the ones you've seen countless pictures of, are clustered on and near the west end of the Mall, right by the Potomac and the Tidal Basin. Let's start with the tallest.

Washington Monument

You can see it from almost anywhere downtown. This 555-foot, 5-1/8 inch marble shaft (named for guess who) dominates the city. It's very simple, but the shape has great power—like an arrow pointing to the heavens. Some people think the little windows at the top look like eyes. The staircase inside has 898 steps, but you aren't allowed to climb them anymore, probably because so many people got exhausted doing it. The elevator takes a mere 70 seconds to whisk you from base to tip, but if you want to make the trip it's best to go first thing in the morning or in the evening when everyone else is having dinner (the floodlit Capitol and city are quite a sight at night).

So what's up there? A great view in all directions. If you don't particularly care about seeing

About 150 feet up from the base, the stone of the monument changes color. This is because construction was stopped for 22 years between 1854 and 1876 because of lack of funds, political infighting, and the Civil War. When it resumed, the stone available was of a slightly different shade.

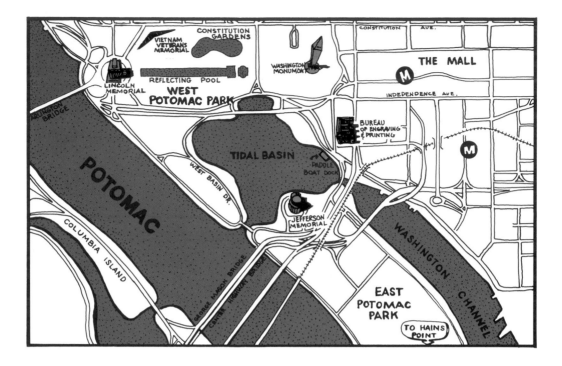

it, don't brave the crowds. If you just want to get up high but haven't the patience for the wait, go to the Old Post Office building in Federal Triangle and zip up the Clock Tower. There's a great view from there, too.

Lincoln Memorial

The Memorial was dedicated in 1922, after seven years of construction.

This monument has an intimate feeling in spite of its size. The magnificent 19-foot-high statue of Lincoln is big, yes, but its power comes more from what a strong sense it gives of what this man was like. He looks thoughtful, a little tired, but also kind and compassionate. His whole body radiates dignity and strength, but quietly instead of in the obvious heroic way of many statues. Now read his words on the marble walls. "Four score and seven years ago..." These are the opening lines of the Gettysburg Address. You probably know them well, but it is a sure bet they will mean more to you here than they ever did before.

Something most people don't know: at certain times of the year, you can tour the area underneath the monument. Interest in this "basement" area perked up about the time of the Bicentennial and exploded when the supermarket tabloid *The National Enquirer* ran a story, "The Ghost that Lives Under the Lincoln Memorial," complete with pictures (not of the ghost, though).

It is dark and musty down there, with massive pillars looming overhead. A guide with a flashlight will lead the way. The original workmen decorated the support columns with all sorts of graffiti, some of which you can see. Because of water seepage, the foundation under the front steps and plaza has developed spiky roof and floor formations (stalactites and stalagmites) exactly like those in a natural cave. The drip-drip you hear means that they're still growing.

Vietnam Veterans Memorial

A sunken V-shaped wall of highly polished black granite designed by 21-year-old student Maya Lin and dedicated in 1982, it is inscribed with the names of all 58,000 Americans killed or missing in the Vietnam War, arranged in order of date of casualty and grouped by year. At first you may think, "So what? It's just a wall." Wait. Vietnam was a very recent war. Your father may have fought in it, or certainly your parents know someone who did. And the people who knew those whose names are written here come every

People tend to be quiet in the Lincoln Memorial because the place has such a strong effect on them.

It's interesting to note that although this memorial stands on government land, the push to build it came mostly from private citizens and veterans themselves, all of whom were determined that those who died in Vietnam would be remembered, even though the war had not been a popular one in many parts of the country.

day and night to bring flowers, letters, and American flags to their dear ones. Some who visit are in uniform themselves. Some cry. Others stand silently, remembering, or ask a Park employee to make a rubbing of a special name to take away with them. After just a few minutes of watching this continuous, quiet drama you begin to get a vivid sense of the human cost of war: the pain, the loss, the bewilderment.

Jefferson Memorial

Completed in 1943, this graceful domed monument to the author of the Declaration of Independence and our third president is quite simple. It is basically one big circular room with a 19-foot statue of Jefferson in the middle and quotations from his writings inscribed on the surrounding walls. The statue does not have the presence of the one in the Lincoln Memorial, but the words are every bit as powerful. Consider coming at night, when the view across the Tidal Basin to the city is very striking.

Bureau of Printing and Engraving

This big gray building near the Tidal Basin is where all the nation's paper money is printed. Enter from the 14th Street side—this is where the tour begins. It is self-guided, so you can go at your own pace. But beware: this is a popular place, and in the summer very crowded, so there may be a wait. As you walk through the building you'll understand the crush. Where else can you see forklifts full of crisp new bills? Thousands of dollars zipping through printing presses right underneath your nose? More than 18 million bills are printed here each day; it's as close as most of us will get to that amount of money in our lives. The bureau also prints passports, government certificates, and all the nation's stamps, but it is the green stuff that is the big draw. If you really want to pretend you are rich, buy a bag of shredded money at the end of the tour for a fraction of what it was worth when it was intact.

East Potomac Park/West Potomac Park/ Hains Point

Tired of pavement? Want to run, stretch out on the grass, watch a game of polo or rugby? In West Potomac Park you can do all those things. Paddle boats are for rent at the Tidal Basin if you want to get out on the water: a big dock sits just down the hill from the Bureau of Printing and Engraving.

East Potomac Park takes up where West Potomac Park leaves off. There is a golf course here as well as places to swim and play tennis. Be

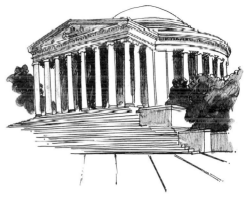

Thomas Jefferson died on July 4, 1826, fifty years to the day after the Declaration of Independence, which he drafted, was adopted by the young American nation.

The design of the building resembles that of buildings Jefferson himself designed (he was an architect as well as a writer and statesman).

sure and drive (you can bike or hike, but it's pretty far) out to Hains Point, where the Potomac and Anacostia rivers meet. There is usually a breeze and lots of boat life on the water. You can watch planes approach and take off from National Airport over in Virginia, have a picnic under big trees, or climb and swing in the playground (it's a good one). The most unusual thing there, though, is *The Awakening*, a statue of a half-buried giant who looks as if he is struggling to break out of the ground and might succeed at any second.

8. Downtown Washington

What most people think of as downtown Washington lies just to the north of the Mall. It's a lot like the downtowns of many cities (office buildings, department stores, traffic), but there are a bunch of things there that you'll be interested in seeing. Let's start with the most famous.

The White House

This is really a judgment call. Everyone will tell you to visit the White House—after all, it's where the president lives. Who knows? If you're lucky, you might even catch a glimpse of him. Well, if you like old houses and are willing to stand in line for anywhere from a half-hour to two hours (depending on the time of year) to see what amounts to five rooms (OK, they *are* famous rooms) then by all means take the White House tour. But if this doesn't appeal to you, take a good look at the building from both sides and forget about it.

Lafayette Park

Across the street from the north side of the White House is a pretty little square called Lafayette Park after the French Revolutionary

Some things you should know about the White House even if you don't go inside: every president except Washington has lived there (and he chose the site). Like the Capitol, the White House was burned by the British in 1814 and had to be rebuilt. Legend has it that the name "White House" came from the thick white paint used to cover the fire damage; it became the official name in 1900.

The Ten Most Wanted Criminals list was started in 1958. Since then, 420 people have been on the list and 393 of those have been caught. The longest anyone has been on the list was 18 years; the shortest, two hours.

In the early days of its history, the White House was open to everyone. Once, when Martin Van Buren was president, a drunk passed out on a sofa and spent the night.

War hero. It has a statue of Andrew Jackson in its center and four more statues (one of Lafayette) placed one in each corner. Like most parks, this one is full of flowers, trees, birds, and squirrels. Unfortunately, these days it is also "home" to a number of homeless people, some of whom you will see sleeping on the benches.

The FBI Tour

This tour has the impact of a good crime show. The exhibits at the start are riveting: John Dillinger's death mask, a clip of a spy surveillance tape, the "Ten Most Wanted" list. The guides seem to have the answer to any question you can think of, plus all sorts of detailed stories to go with the displays.

Next are the crime labs. You can watch technicians type blood samples, scrutinize handwriting, and analyze fibers and paint chips. There is a room with 4,200(!) guns and another with 12,000 different kinds of bullets and cartridges. All this ends with a literal bang. At tour's end you're taken downstairs to the agency's indoor firing range where an agent gives a shooting demonstration with a .357 Magnum, a 9mm pistol, and a submachine gun. If you're into firearms, this is the place for you. If you're not, go anyway. It's one of the liveliest shows in town.

The Old Post Office

You'll recognize it by the clock tower. Not long ago this wonderfully ornate nineteenth-century building (nicknamed "The Old Tooth") was slated for demolition. Today, it's a combination office building and indoor pavilion plus mall. There are lots of places here to grab lunch or a

40

snack; you can get almost any kind of food you want. After noshing, take a stroll around the main floor and browse in the shops. Finally, take the elevator to the top of the clock tower and enjoy the view. Also up here are ten great bells, a gift from Britain for the Bicentennial. They are rung on holidays and ceremonial occasions.

The main floor was where mail was sorted in the old days.

Other Things to See and Do Downtown

For a change of pace, visit the **National Aquarium** in the Department of Commerce building on 14th Street. It's small but surprisingly comprehensive, with fish from all over the world and exhibits that tell you about their habits and habitats. A "touch tank" has crabs, sea urchins, and other water creatures that you can feel. Another attraction, feeding the sharks and piranhas, happens several times a week.

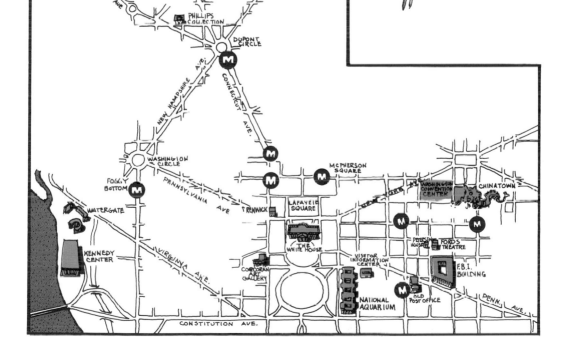

A good time to visit is late February, when the Chinese New Year is celebrated with parades and other festivities.

Just up the street from the FBI Building is **Ford's Theater**, where Lincoln was shot by John Wilkes Booth in 1865. It has been restored to the way it appeared that fateful night and is now a museum as well as a theater. Across the street is the **Petersen House**, where the wounded president was carried and where he died. This, too, is now a museum. Both are sobering places to visit: it's as if some of the sadness from that long-ago time still lingers.

A huge carved red gate at 7th and H streets, N.W., welcomes you to **Chinatown**. It's not very big (just a couple of blocks square), but it has restaurants where you can get *dim sum* (small turnoverlike pastries with meat or vegetable filling) and some wonderfully dark, musty "general stores" full of Oriental treasures. There's a great one by the gate that sells samurai swords. Street signs are in both Chinese and English. Another ethnic neighborhood is **Adams-Morgan**, a Latin-American enclave between Connecticut and Florida avenues. Colorful festivals take place here at various times of the year, and there are lots of ethnic restaurants as well.

Some more museums: the **Corcoran**, with an outstanding collection of European and American art (there are beautiful works by Mary Cassatt and Winslow Homer), and the **Renwick**, which emphasizes crafts—textiles, glass, unusual objects you will want to touch (unfortunately, you can't, but there's a great gift shop with similar things that you can buy). Near Dupont Circle is the **Phillips Collection**, strong on modern art though not limited to it. This museum was once the private home of its founder and feels very different from other galleries.

North of the Lincoln Memorial on the Potomac is the **Kennedy Center for the Performing Arts**, a huge marble rectangle surrounded by pillars. Dedicated in 1971, this cultural center offers theater, opera, and music of all sorts.

Nearby is a large curved building containing upscale shops, offices, apartments, and a hotel. This is the **Watergate** where, in 1972, five men were caught breaking into the headquarters of the Democratic National Committee. This burglary started a chain of events that culminated in 1974 with the resignation of President Nixon. Give a cheer for democracy as you drive past—not many nations could endure the turmoil this one did for two years and emerge with its constitutional system of government intact.

American Ballet Theater performs here, and there's a resident opera company and orchestra.

9. Georgetown and Points Northwest

orthwest of downtown, across Rock Creek and the park that shares its name (more about them later), lies **Georgetown**, one of Washington's best-known neighborhoods. Actually, Georgetown was a bustling city before the capital was even thought of. Today it is an area of beautiful old homes as well as a thriving commercial district full of restaurants, art galleries, and trendy shops.

A good place to start exploring Georgetown is at the intersection of the area's two main streets, M and Wisconsin. There is a very definite street scene here, especially at night and on the weekends, so if you don't like crowds don't stay long. If you like shopping, though, you've found your spot. Georgetown is a consumer's paradise. If you've got limited time, try **Georgetown Park** at 3222 M Street, an elegant three-story indoor mall with restaurants, hip stores like the Limited, and even a branch of F.A.O. Schwartz (perhaps the world's best toy store). If you're into punk, try **Commander Salamander** (1420 Wisconsin Ave.) for weird glasses, T-shirts, and Spandex. **Urban Outfitters** on M near Wisconsin offers slightly more subdued but definitely new-wave clothing.

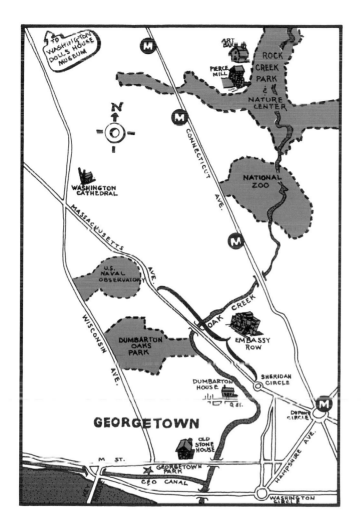

Step down the street from Urban Outfitters, with its funky jackets and loud rock music, to the **Old Stone House**. You've just entered another world—the world of 200 years ago. No radios, TV, VCRs, or even electric lights. Just a rough, simple, stone house with low ceilings, small rooms, and handmade furniture. This house, thought to be the only pre-Revolutionary

War building in the whole District (it was built in 1765), is furnished as it was in the late eighteenth century and staffed by men and women in period dress. In back is a lovely large garden with fruit trees and flowers; it's a popular local spot for a picnic lunch.

Down the hill from M Street you'll find the old Chesapeake and Ohio (C&O) canal next to the river. Started in 1829, it was originally supposed to link Washington with Pittsburgh. But the project turned out to be too ambitious and expensive, and once it reached Cumberland, Maryland, 185 miles to the west, construction was halted. Today it's a park, and hikers, bikers, and joggers use its paths for fun and exercise.

You can get a taste of what it was like on the old C&O by taking a ride on a mule-drawn canal boat. In spring, summer, and fall, *The Georgetown* makes several trips a day. It is a pretty, peaceful one-and-a-half hour trip. The pace is slow. Trees arch over the canal as you drift past quaint old houses and see people strolling by the water. Boatmen in period dress work the boat through a lock while they tell stories and sing songs.

Once you get away from Wisconsin Avenue and M Street, Georgetown changes character and becomes much more of a "town." On some tree-lined blocks you can imagine you are living one hundred years ago, or even two. Some streets are still cobblestoned. There are many beautiful old homes to look at. Two that are open to the public are **Dumbarton House** (built in 1799) at 2715 Q Street, N.W., and **Dumbarton Oaks**, at 1703 32nd Street, N.W. Dumbarton Oaks is also a museum with noted collections of Byzantine and pre-Columbian art and a famous garden.

There is a similar trip that starts at Great Falls, Maryland, much farther to the west. The scenery there is much wilder and more dramatic.

The National Zoo

By all means, don't miss the zoo. It's one of the world's best. Here is one place where you don't feel sorry for the animals. Their enclosures have been landscaped to resemble where they live in the wild and blend in beautifully with the land around them. Beavers have a stream and dam; lions a shaded, stony hill with a moat. Where there are cages, they are big, big, big. The two-story outdoor Flight Cage swoops up next to the Bird House. Inside, the birds have plenty of room to fly, and you can walk through and watch them. The gibbon cage is another big mesh structure set in a group of trees and filled with climbing devices. A few feet from your nose, chattering monkeys swing up, down, and sideways.

Dumbarton Oaks was also the site, in 1944, of the conference that marked the beginning of the United Nations.

Founded in 1889, the zoo occupies 163 leafy, hilly acres in Rock Creek Park. About 4,000 animals live here, representing 500 species.

There are six trails winding through the zoo, each one color-coded for a certain animal group. Follow them if you want to structure your visit; if not, just wander. Be sure not to miss the zoo's most famous residents, the giant pandas Hsing-Hsing (male) and Ling-Ling (female)—you'll want to take them home with you.

Pay a visit to the big orange orangutan who looks like Jabba the Hut. The Reptile House, too, merits a look-see. Here, in addition to looking at all kinds of snakes and toads, you can visit **Herplab**, a learning center for young people. Available in other parts of the zoo are **Birdlab** and **Zoolab**, which have hands-on exhibits. They're interesting, but the real draw here is the animals.

Unfortunately, pandas are disappearing in the wild. The cages of other species in the zoo that are threatened with extinction are marked ''Vanishing Animal.''

There is also a nineteenth-century tearoom where, if you plan ahead, you can have your birthday party.

Washington Dolls' House and Toy Museum

A little out of the way (it's up in Chevy Chase near the District line—take a cab) but well worth the trip. The small yellow and white clapboard house contains a treasury of old toys, dolls, and the most detailed, elaborate miniature homes you'll ever see. The houses come from all over the United States and Europe. There is even a huge nineteenth-century Mexican hacienda with a garage, ornamental grillwork, and frosted glass doors. Upstairs are two shops. One is filled with all sorts of miniature furniture, dolls, and things that a doll might need, like a little Christmas tree or a tiny jack-'o-lantern; the other stocks supplies for the dolls' house builder.

National Cathedral

Although it is technically Protestant (Episcopal), this is a church for people from all faiths. You can see its 697-foot tower from miles away, as the cathedral sits on top of Mt. St. Alban, one of the two highest points of land in the District (the other is Jenkins Hill, site of the Capitol). Started in 1907 and still not finished, this huge medieval-style church is laid out in the shape of a cross. All is quiet as you enter. A hundred feet above you soars a vast arched roof, flanked by the flags of the 50 states, and stained glass windows, one of which celebrates the Apollo XI space flight (it even has a piece of moon rock embedded in the glass). Light streams down from three huge rose windows; the altar stands in front of you. It's both very grand and very peaceful—a good place to listen to your heart.

Embassy Row

Many foreign governments have representatives in Washington, and the mansions where many of them live and work are clustered along Massachusetts Avenue north from Sheridan Square to the U.S. Naval Observatory. This area is worth driving past, maybe on your way to the zoo or the National Cathedral. Most of the embassies are well marked on the outside and fly their national flags. Look for the elephant statues in front of the Indian Embassy and the spire of the Mosque and Islamic Center.

Rock Creek Park and Nature Center

Here are 1,754 acres of woodland and field that snake through the heart of Washington from the Potomac northward, following the stream it takes its name from. Here you can bike, hike, play tennis or baseball, picnic—in short, have just about any kind of outdoor fun imaginable. There's a nature center toward the north of the park, with exhibits on the native forest and wildlife, plus a planetarium and nature trails.

Also in the Cathedral complex: a lovely, small-scale Children's Chapel, an exceptional gift shop, and the London Brass Rubbing Center (relocating in early 1989; call [202] 364-0030 for new location), where you can make your own reproduction of any one of 65 medieval brasses. Just place your paper on top of the design and then rub with a special wax-based metallic stick. The attendant will help you. As you rub, the picture appears. You may want to do several

10. Virginia

The original plan for Washington called for a square 10 miles on a side. Some of this designated 100-square-mile area was on the south side of the Potomac. The city grew so slowly that in 1846 Congress gave that land back to Virginia.

The cemetery covers 612 acres.

A number of things to see in Washington are actually not in Washington at all. They're in Virginia, just across the Potomac River.

Arlington National Cemetery
This is just across the Arlington Memorial Bridge from the Lincoln Memorial. Here more than 200,000 military veterans and their wives and children lie buried, along with other distinguished Americans. The cemetery affects visitors in much the same way as the Vietnam Veterans Memorial: it, too, makes visible the human cost of war. The gently rolling grass is covered as far as the eye can see with plain white stones, each with a name on it, most marking a life lost in the service and defense of this country. It's hard to take freedom for granted in the company of so many who died to preserve it.

There are larger memorials here as well. The **Tomb of the Unknowns** holds the remains of anonymous dead from four wars; soldiers stand guard before it 24 hours a day (for a stirring display of military pomp and precision, watch the changing of the guard every half-hour; every two hours at night). One of the most moving

50

memorials is the one to **President John F. Kennedy**, assassinated in 1963. His simple grave, marked by an eternal flame and flanked by the graves of two of his children who died in infancy, has personal significance for many who visit. They remember him, and they remember the horror of his death. Nearby is the plain stone, engraved with just a name and dates, that covers the grave of his brother, Robert, also shot down by an assassin.

Just north of Arlington Cemetery is the **Marine Corps War Memorial**, popularly known as the Iwo Jima statue. It honors fallen members of the Marine Corps. This massive sculpture is based on a famous photograph taken after the capture of the Pacific island of Iwo Jima from the Japanese during World War II. Six marines (here, four times bigger than life) struggle to raise an American flag in victory. Note that while the men are made of bronze, the flag is gloriously real. Nearby stands the **Netherlands Carillon**, a slender tower capped with bells given to this country as a thank-you by the Dutch after the Second World War.

Near the Iwo Jima statue lies **Theodore**

Some notable Americans who are buried at Arlington include President William Howard Taft; heavyweight boxing champion Joe Louis; Supreme Court Justices Oliver Wendell Holmes, William O. Douglas, and Earl Warren; Pierre L'Enfant, planner of the city of Washington; Robert E. Peary and Richard Byrd, Arctic explorers.

Roosevelt Island, 88 acres of woods, swamp, and wildlife refuge in the middle of the Potomac dedicated to the memory of a president who was a great outdoorsman. You get there via a footbridge from the Virginia side of the river: no cars are allowed. It is a great place to hike and pretend you are miles from civilization.

The Pentagon

This imposing five-sided edifice, near Arlington Cemetery and just across the 14th Street bridge from downtown Washington, houses the Department of Defense (meaning the Army, Navy, Air Force, and Marine Corps bureaucracies and that of the Joint Chiefs of Staff). No wonder the military budget is so big. The tour here (you can't see the building any other way) includes a film and much war memorabilia.

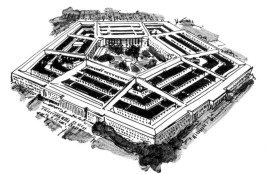

The Pentagon is the world's largest office building, with 17.5 miles of corridors and 3.7 million square feet of office space.

Just south of Arlington on the Potomac (but still on the Metro line) is the town of **Alexandria**. Like Georgetown, this city was a thriving port long before Washington was founded. The area of the city near the river is called Oldtown. Like Georgetown, it has many historic homes, restaurants, and trendy shops catering to tourists. A pretty place with cobblestone streets and old-time charm, but not that different from stuff you may have seen elsewhere. If you do visit, check out the **Torpedo Factory**, where you can watch painters and sculptors at work.

Mt. Vernon

This was George Washington's plantation home on the bank of the Potomac River, sixteen miles south of Washington. If you only visit one old house on your trip, visit this one.

Mt. Vernon is one of the most visited places in the United States, so try and get there when the gates first open. What you see first are rolling fields. Remember, this was a working plantation. In Washington's day, it contained five farms stretching over 8,000 acres. Walk up a gentle slope, past gardens and big old trees, to the main house, which sits on a rise overlooking the river. The view from the sweeping lawn down to the water is much as it was 200 years ago.

This graceful, white, two-story building is definitely worth walking through. The rooms and their furnishings, most of which are as they were in the 1700s, give you a real sense of how Washington and his family lived. Indeed, in spite of its many visitors, all of Mt. Vernon gives you

You can get to Mt. Vernon by car (it's a pretty drive), by bus, by Tourmobile in the summer, or, from March to late autumn, by boat. **The Spirit of Mt. Vernon** *makes daily 1½ hour trips from Pier 4 at 6th and Water streets, S.W.; it's a scenic, leisurely way to go. If you are really feeling energetic, rent a bike. There is a cycling and jogging path next to the highway which runs all the way from Washington.*

an uncanny sense of being in the past. It also gives you a feeling for Washington the man as opposed to Washington the national hero. The simple beauty and dignity of the buildings and grounds reflect a man who had those qualities as well—a man who, when he was away serving his country, always wanted to come back here and just be a farmer. Fittingly, he and his wife, Martha, are buried here. Their unpretentious tomb sits in the woods down the hill toward the wharf.

The many outbuildings of the estate are almost more interesting than the main house. The kitchen, the smokehouse, the stables all give you a glimpse of what eighteenth-century plantation life must have been like. Especially enlightening (and disturbing) are the slaves' quarters, where several families cooked, ate, and slept in one dark room.

During his life, Washington came to oppose slavery and, in his will, freed his 125 slaves.

11. Excursions

There is enough to do in the city of Washington itself to keep you busy for weeks. However, if you have got a car, some extra time, and are itching to get out in the countryside, here are some suggestions for day trips in the metropolitan area.

Great Falls of the Potomac

Here at the west end of MacArthur Boulevard in Maryland, about ten miles from downtown D.C., the river drops 50 crashing, splashing feet. The 800-acre park around the falls has miles and miles of trails. Don't forget the C&O Canal—it's here, too.

At Pierce Mill, a restored grist mill, you can see how flour used to be made. There are art classes and exhibits at the Art Barn next door.

Claude Moore Colonial Farm at Turkey Run, McLean, Virginia

This is a working model of a poor homestead of colonial times. The 100-acre farm is worked by its "family" as it would have been in the 1770s, using identical tools and agricultural methods.

Oxon Hill Farm, Oxon Hill, Maryland

Another farm, this one depicting life in the early 1900s. Watch cider being made, sheep being shorn, and other farm activities.

Ft. Washington

An 1814 fort across the Potomac from Mt. Vernon, with lots of places to run and climb. Bring a picnic.

Goddard Space Flight Center Visitor Center and Museum

If the National Air and Space Museum wasn't enough for you, make the trip up to Greenbelt, Maryland, and see more exhibits about the space program. Lots of rockets. Run by NASA.

Wolf Trap Farm, Vienna, Virginia

This is the only national park devoted to the performing arts. Here you can try your hand at theater, puppetry, mime, and dance; visit the yearly International Children's Festival; see performances of all kinds and do regular park things like picnic and run around in the woods. Call to see what's happening when you're in the area ([703] 255-1900).

12. Now That Your Trip Is Over

Well, now your trip to Washington is almost over. Chances are your legs ache from walking so much and you could use an extra suitcase for all the pamphlets, postcards, T-shirts, and general stuff you have picked up along the way. Chances are, too, that your head is spinning with all the sights you've seen and the new experiences you've had. History has come alive; government seems much less stuffy. Maybe a picture at the National Gallery made you see things a little differently, or the graves at Arlington brought you unexpectedly near tears. Perhaps it will be the view from the top of the Washington Monument or all those rockets at the Air and Space Museum that you will remember when you look back. Whatever it is, there is bound to be something from this trip that sticks with you for a long time.

The great thing about Washington, too, is that it improves every time you visit. New attractions are always springing up, and the old standbys, like the Lincoln Memorial, get better and better, like old friends. So when you leave, don't say good-bye. Say "See you soon!" and plan to come back.

Calendar

January

First Monday, opening of Congress.

Third Monday, Martin Luther King, Jr. birthday celebrations.

Jan. 18: Robert E. Lee birthday celebration. Candlelight tours of his boyhood home in Alexandria.

Jan. 20: every fourth year, Presidential inauguration.

February

Feb. 12: Abraham Lincoln's birthday. Festivities at Lincoln Memorial.

Feb. 22: Washington's birthday. Festivities at Washington Monument, Alexandria, and Mt. Vernon.

Late Feb.: Chinese New Year. Celebrations in Chinatown.

March

Mar. 14: St. Patrick's Day. Parade down Constitution Avenue.

Late Mar.: Smithsonian Kite Festival on the Mall.

Late Mar./early Apr.: The circus comes to town.

April

Easter Egg Roll, White House lawn.

Easter Services, Arlington National Cemetery.

National Cherry Blossom Festival: Fireworks, music, parades, even a marathon.

Imagination Celebration: Annual performing arts festival for young people at the Kennedy Center.

Apr. 13: Thomas Jefferson's birthday. Festivities at the Jefferson Memorial.

White House spring garden tour.

May

Goodwill Embassy Tour Days. Various foreign embassies open their doors.

Greek Spring Festival.

Malcolm X Day.

Memorial Day: National Symphony Concert on grounds of the Capitol, wreath laying at Arlington and Vietnam Veterans Memorial.

All Summer Long

Free outdoor military band concerts at various places on the Mall held almost every evening.

Marine Corps Friday evening parades, Marine Barracks, 8th and I streets, S.E.

Parades and music on the Ellipse every Wednesday night.

Artists, mimes, musicians, and dancers perform weekends on the Mall.

June

Alexandria Waterfront Festival.

Smithsonian Festival of American Folklife on the Mall.

Potomac Riverfest.

Smithsonian Boomerang Festival, Washington Monument grounds.

July

Jul. 4: Independence Day festivities on the Mall. Fireworks, music, parades.

Mostly Mozart Festival, Kennedy Center.

Hispanic/American Cultural Festival, Adams-Morgan and Mt. Pleasant neighborhoods.

August

Annual "1812 Overture" Concert, U.S. Army Band.

Navy Band Lollipop Concert for young people.

Renaissance Fair, Annapolis, Maryland.

Football season (the Redskins) starts.

September

Annual National Frisbee Festival, the Mall.

Labor Day weekend: International Children's Festival, Wolf Trap Farm Park, Vienna, Va.

Reggae Festival.

Croquet Tournament, the Ellipse.

Adams-Morgan Day: Hispanic festivities.

Rock Creek Park Day: Music, food, arts and crafts.

October

First Monday: Supreme Court convenes.

Columbus Day festivities.

White House fall garden tour.

International Horse Show, Landover, Md.

Washington Cathedral, open house.

November

Veterans Day: Services in Arlington National Cemetery.

Early Nov.: Washington's Review of the Troops. Reenactment of colonial scene at Gadsby's Tavern, Alexandria.

Marine Corps Marathon.

December

The city is full of Christmas cheer. There are lights and trees everywhere and caroling and other festivities almost every night on the Mall.

Scottish Christmas Walk, Alexandria, Va. Parade, bagpipes, dancing, children's events.

Lighting of National and White House Christmas trees.

"The Nutcracker Suite" at the Kennedy Center.

Annual Poinsettia Show, U.S. Botanic Gardens.

New Year's Eve celebration at the Old Post Office.

For additional, up-to-the-minute information, check the local papers or call the Washington Convention and Visitors Association at (202)789-7000.

Appendix

Arthur M. Sackler Gallery
1058 Independence Avenue, S.W.
(202)357-2700; 357-2020 Dial-A-Museum
recording
Hours: 10 a.m.–5:30 p.m. daily. Closed December
25. Extended summer hours determined annually. Admission free.

Art and Industries Building of the Smithsonian
Institution
900 Jefferson Drive, S.W.
(202)357-2700; 357-2020 Dial-A-Museum
recording
Hours: 10 a.m.–5:30 p.m. daily. Closed December
25. Extended summer hours determined annually. For information on Discovery Theater, call
(202)357-1500. Admission free.

Arlington House
Arlington National Cemetery, Arlington, Va.
(703)629-0931
Hours: 9:30 a.m.–6 p.m. daily, Apr.–Sept.; 9:30
a.m.–4:30 p.m. Oct.–Mar. Closed December 25,
January 1. Admission free.

Arlington National Cemetery
Arlington, Va. (703)629-0931
Hours: 8 a.m.–7 p.m. daily, Apr.–Sept.; 8 a.m.–5
p.m. daily, Oct.–Mar. Admission free.

Bureau of Engraving and Printing
14th and C Streets, S.W. (202)447-0193
Hours: 9 a.m.–2 p.m., Mon.–Fri. Admission free.

Capital Children's Museum
800 Third Street, N.E.
(202)543-8600; MET-KIDS
Hours: 10 a.m.–5 p.m. daily. Closed Thanksgiving, December 25, January 1, and Easter. Admission: $4.00. Senior citizens, $1.00. Members and
children under 2 free.

**Chesapeake and Ohio (C&O) Canal National
Historic Park**
Along the Potomac from Rock Creek West

Boat ride tickets and information: *The Geor-
getown* at Foundry Mall, 1055 Jefferson Street,
N.W., (202)472-4276. *The Canal Clipper* at Great
Falls Tavern, 11710 MacArthur Boulevard,
Potomac, Md., (301)299-2026. Boats run from late
April through mid-October.

Claude Moore Colonial Farm at Turkey Run
6310 Georgetown Pike, McLean, Va.
(703)442-7557
Hours: 10 a.m.–4:30 p.m. Wed.–Sat., Apr.–Dec.
Closed during bad weather and on Thanksgiving
and December 25. Admission: $1.00 adults; $0.50
children. Members free.

Corcoran Gallery of Art
17th and New York Avenue, N.W. (202)638-3211
Hours: 10 a.m.–4:30 p.m. Tues.–Sat. Closed Monday, some major holidays. Admission free.

Dumbarton House
2715 Q Street, N.W. (202)337-2288
Hours: 9 a.m.–12:30 p.m. Mon.–Sat. Closed Sundays, holidays, and all of August. Admission free
but donations welcome.

Dumbarton Oaks Gardens and Museum
1703 32nd Street, N.W. (202)342-3200
Hours: Gardens open daily 2 p.m.–5 p.m. Nov.–
Mar.; 2 p.m.–6 p.m. Apr.–Oct. Collection open 2
p.m.–5 p.m., Tues.–Sun. Admission: Adults
$2.00; seniors and children $1.00 (Apr.–Oct.).
Free Nov.–Mar.

Eastern Market
7th and C Streets S.E. (near N. Carolina Avenue)
Hours: 7 a.m.–6 p.m. Tues.–Thurs.; 6 a.m.–7 p.m.
Fri.–Sat.

Federal Bureau of Investigation (FBI)
J. Edgar Hoover Bldg., Pennsylvania Ave. between
9th and 10th Streets, N.W. (202)324-3447
Hours: Guided one-hour tours leave every 15-20
minutes from E Street entrance, 8:45 a.m.–4:15
p.m. Mon.–Fri. Closed Sat., Sun., holidays.
Admission free.

Folger Shakespeare Library

201 E. Capitol St., S.E. (202)544-7077 library;
546-4000 theater box office
Hours: 10 a.m.–4 p.m. Mon.–Sat.; tours 11
a.m.–1 p.m. Closed Sundays and holidays. Admission free for library; tickets required for evening events.

Ford's Theater

511 10th Street, N.W. (202)426-6924 museum;
347-4833 box office
Hours: 9 a.m.–5 p.m. daily. Talks given in theater
about the assassination hourly, 9:30 a.m.–4:30
p.m. Closed December 25. Theater closed on
rehearsal days and one hour before matinees.
Admission: $1.00 for theater. Museum free.

Fort Washington

Ft. Washington Rd., Oxon Hill, Md.
(301)763-4600
Hours: 8:30 a.m.–5 p.m. daily. Closed December
25, January 1. Admission free.

Freer Gallery of Art

Jefferson Drive at 12th Street, S.W.
(202)357-2700; 357-2020 Dial-A-Museum
recording
Closed for renovation until 1991.
Hours (when open): 10 a.m.–5:30 p.m. daily.
Closed December 25. Expanded summer hours
determined annually. Admission free.

Glen Echo Park

Goldsboro Road and MacArthur Blvd., Glen Echo,
Md. (301)492-6282 information; Adventure Theater (301)320-5331; park (301)492-6229
Hours: Carousel (May-Sept.): 10 a.m.–2 p.m.
Wed.–Sun.; noon–6 p.m. Sat.–Sun. Art gallery:
noon–5 p.m. Tues.–Sun.; closed Mondays and
holidays.

Goddard Visitor Center and Museum

Greenbelt, Md. (301)286-8103
Hours: 10 a.m.–4 p.m. Wed.–Sun. Admission
free.

Great Falls Park

9200 Old Dominion Drive, Great Falls, Va.
(703)285-2965
Hours: 8 a.m.–dusk. Admission: $3.00 per vehicle; $2.00 per pedestrian.

Hirshhorn Museum and Sculpture Garden

Independence Avenue at 8th Street, S.W.
(202)357-2700; 357-2020 Dial-A-Museum
recording
Hours: 10 a.m.–5:30 p.m. daily. Closed December
25. Extended summer hours determined annually. Sculpture garden open daily 7:30 a.m.–dusk.
Admission free.

Jefferson Memorial

South Bank of Tidal Basin, West Potomac Park
(202)426-6821
Always open. Admission free.

John F. Kennedy Center for the Performing Arts

New Hampshire Ave. and Rock Creek Parkway,
N.W. (202)254-3600; 857-0900 box office
Hours: 10 a.m.–10 p.m. daily. Tours 10 a.m.–1
p.m. Admission free; tickets required for evening
performances.

Library of Congress

Jefferson Bldg., First St. and E. Capitol St., S.E.;
John Adams Annex, Second St. and Independence
Ave., S.E.; Madison Bldg., 101 Independence Ave.,
S.E. (202)287-5000
Hours: Exhibit areas open 8:30 a.m.–5:30 p.m.,
Mon.–Fri. Madison Gallery, Great Hall and lower
level of Jefferson Bldg. open 8:30 a.m.–9:30 p.m.,
Mon.–Fri.; 8:30 a.m.–6 p.m., Sat.–Sun.
45-minute tours begin at Orientation Theater in
Jefferson Bldg., 9 a.m.–4 p.m., Mon.–Fri. Admission free.

Lincoln Memorial

West End of Mall (202)426-6895
Always open. Admission free. Tour of foundations weekends in spring and fall. Call six weeks
in advance for reservations.

London Brass Rubbing Center

Call (202)364-0030 for location and hours.

Metro

Stations marked by "M" sign. Metro Center, the
central link for all lines, is at 11th and G streets,
N.W. (202)637-2437 for information.
Hours: Trains run 6 a.m.–midnight, Mon.–Fri.; 8
a.m.–midnight, Sat.; 10 a.m.–midnight, Sun.
Fare dependent on destination.

Mount Vernon

Mt. Vernon, Va. (703)780-2000
Hours: 9 a.m.–4 p.m., Nov.–Feb.; 9 a.m.–5 p.m.,
Mar.-Oct. Admission: Adults, $5.00; over 61,
$4.00; ages 6-11, $2.00.

National Air and Space Museum

Independence Avenue between 3rd and 7th
Streets, N.W. (202)357-2700; 357-2020 Dial-A-
Museum recording
Hours: 10 a.m.–5:30 p.m. daily. Closed December
25. Extended summer hours determined annually. Admission free.

National Aquarium

Dept. of Commerce Bldg., 14th St. and Constitution Avenue, N.W. (202)337-2825
Hours: 9 a.m.–5 p.m. daily. Closed December 25.
Shark feeding Mon., Wed., Sat. at 2 p.m.; piranha

feeding Tues., Thurs., Sat. at 2 p.m. Admission free.

National Archives
Constitution Avenue and 8th Street, N.W. (202)523-3000
Hours: Exhibition hall open 10 a.m.–5:30 p.m. daily. Closed December 25. Extended summer hours determined annually. Admission free.

National Cathedral (Cathedral Church of St. Peter and St. Paul)
Mt. St. Alban at Massachusetts and Wisconsin Avenues, N.W. (202)537-6200
Hours: 10 a.m.–4:30 p.m., Mon.–Sat.; 8 a.m.–4:30 p.m., Sun. Tours 10 a.m.–noon, 1 p.m.–3:15 p.m., Mon.–Sat. Admission free, but donations welcome.

National Gallery of Art
Constitution Avenue between 3rd and 7th Streets, N.W. (202)737-4215
Hours: 10 a.m.–5 p.m., Mon.–Sat.; noon–9 p.m. Sun. Closed December 25, January 1. Extended summer hours determined annually. Admission free.

National Museum of African Art
950 Independence Avenue, S.W. (202)357-2700; 357 2020 Dial-A-Museum recording
Hours: 10 a.m.–5:30 p.m. daily. Closed December 25. Extended summer hours determined annually. Admission free.

National Museum of American History
14th and Constitution Avenue, N.W. (202)357-2700; 357-2020 Dial-A-Museum recording
Hours: 10 a.m.–5:30 p.m. daily. Closed December 25. Extended summer hours determined annually. Admission free.

National Museum of Natural History
10th Street and Constitution Avenue, N.W. (202)357-2700; 357 2020 Dial-A-Museum recording
Hours: 10 a.m.–5:30 p.m. daily. Closed December 25. Extended summer hours determined annually. Discovery Room open noon–2:30 p.m., Mon.–Thurs.; 10:30 a.m.–3:30 p.m., Fri.–Sun. Admission free.

National Zoological Park
3000 block of Connecticut Avenue, N.W. (202)673-4717
Hours: Grounds open 8 a.m.–6 p.m.; buildings 9 a.m.–4:30 p.m., Sept. 16–Apr. 30. Grounds open 8 a.m.–8 p.m., buildings 9 a.m.–6 p.m., May 1–Sept. 15. Closed December 25. ZOOlab, HERP-

lab and BIRDlab open noon–3 p.m., Fri.–Sun. Open additional days Jun. 1–Aug. 30. Admission free.

Old Post Office
Pennsylvania Avenue and 12th Street, N.W. (202)523-5671 tower; 289-4224 pavilion
Hours: 8 a.m.–11 p.m., mid-Apr. to mid-Sept.; 10 a.m.–5:45 p.m., mid-Sept.–mid-Apr. Shops open 10 a.m.–8 p.m., Mon.–Sat.; noon–6 p.m., Sun. Admission free.

Old Stone House
3051 M Street, N.W. (202)426-6871
Hours: 9:30 a.m.–5 p.m., Wed. –Sun. Closed December 25, January 1, and Thanksgiving. Admission free.

Oxon Hill Farm
Oxon Hill, Md. (301)839-1177
Hours: 8:30 a.m.–5 p.m. daily. Closed major holidays. Admission free.

Paul E. Garber Preservation, Restoration and Storage Facility
Suitland, Md. (301)357-1400
Hours: Tours Mon.–Fri. at 10 a.m.; weekends at 10 a.m. and 1 p.m. Reservations must be made two weeks in advance. Closed December 25. Annual open house one weekend in spring. Admission free.

Pentagon
Arlington, Va. (202)545-6700; 695-1776 tours
Hours: 9:30 a.m.–3:30 p.m. for 1¼-hour tour. Closed holidays. Admission free.

Petersen House
516 10th Street, N.W. (202)426-6830
Hours: 9 a.m.–5:00 p.m. daily. Closed December 25. Admission free.

Phillips Collection
1600 21st Street, N.W. (202)387-0961
Hours: 10 a.m.–5 p.m., Tues.–Sat.; 2 p.m.–7 p.m., Sunday. Closed Monday, most major holidays. Admission free, but contributions suggested.

Potomac Parks, East and West
South of Independence Avenue, West of 14th Street (202)426-6700
Always open. Admission free.

Renwick Gallery
Pennsylvania Avenue at 17th Street, N.W. (202)357-2700; 357 2020 Dial-A-Museum recording
Hours: 10 a.m.–5:30 p.m. daily. Closed December 25. Admission free.

Rock Creek Park and Nature Center
5200 Glover Rd., N.W. (202)426-6829 Nature Center; 426-6832 Park Headquarters
Hours: Nature Center open 9:30 a.m.–5 p.m., Tues.–Fri., noon–6 p.m., Sat.–Sun. (Dec.–Apr., noon–5 p.m.) Closed Monday. Admission free

Smithsonian Institution "Castle"
1000 Jefferson Drive S.W. (202)357-2700; 357-2020 Dial-A-Museum recording
Closed until late 1989.
Hours: 10 a.m.–5:30 p.m. daily. Closed December 25. Extended summer hours determined annually. Admission free.

Theodore Roosevelt Island
In Potomac River, off G. Washington Memorial Pkwy (northbound), McLean, Va.
(703)285-2598; 285-2601
Hours: 8 a.m.–dusk. Closed December 25. Admission free.

Torpedo Factory
105 N. Union Street, Alexandria, Va.
(703)838-4565
Hours: 10 a.m.–5 p.m. daily. Closed Thanksgiving, December 25, and January 1. Admission free.

Tourmobile
Tours to Washington, Arlington, Mt. Vernon, Frederick Douglass National Historical Site.
Fares vary. Call (202)554-7980 for information.

Union Station
50 Massachusetts Avenue, N.E.
(202)682-3767; (800)872-7245 Amtrak
Hours: Station open 24 hours. Shops open 10 a.m.–9 p.m., Mon.–Sat.; noon–6 p.m., Sun. Admission free.

U.S. Botanic Garden
First Street and Maryland Avenue, S.W.
(202)225-8333; 225-7099
Hours: 9 a.m.–9 p.m. daily, June–Aug.; 9 a.m.–5 p.m. daily, rest of year. Admission free.

U.S. Capitol
East End of Mall on Capitol Hill
(202)224-3121
Hours: 9 a.m.–4:30 p.m. daily. Extended summer hours. 30-minute guided tours leave from the rotunda 9 a.m.–3:45 p.m. Closed Thanksgiving, December 25, January 1. Passes for House and Senate chambers can be obtained from your representative's or senator's office. Visitors galleries open 9 a.m.–4:30 p.m., or until session adjourns. Admission free.

U.S. Supreme Court
First and E. Capitol Street, S.E. (202)479-3000
Hours: 9 a.m.–4:30 p.m., Mon.–Fri. Court in session from first Monday of October through June. Cases heard 10 a.m.–noon, 1 p.m.–3 p.m., Mon.–Wed. the first two weeks of the month. Monday is usually when decisions are announced. When court is not in session, talks on the operation of the Court are given in the courtroom 9:30 a.m.–3:30 p.m., every hour on the half-hour. Exhibits and film showing on ground floor. Admission free.

Vietnam Veterans Memorial
West End of Mall in Constitution Gardens
(202)426-6700
Always open. Admission free.

Washington Dolls' House and Toy Museum
5236 44th Street, N.W. (Chevy Chase)
(202)244-0024
Hours: 10 a.m.–5 p.m., Tues.–Sat.; noon–5 p.m., Sun. Admission: Adults, $2.00; children under 14, $1.00.

Washington Monument
Center of Mall, Constitution Ave. and 15th St., N.W. (202)426-6839
Hours: 8 a.m.–midnight, Mar. 20–Labor Day; 9 a.m.–5 p.m., rest of year. Tours three times a day in summer; once a day rest of year. Admission free.

Washington Navy Yard and Museum
9th and M Streets, S.E. (202)433-2651
Hours: 9 a.m.–4 p.m., Mon.–Fri.(9 a.m.–5 p.m. in summer); 10 a.m.–5 p.m., Sat., Sun. U.S. Destroyer *Barry* open 10 a.m.–5 p.m. daily. Closed Thanksgiving, December 25, January 1. Admission free.

White House
1600 Pennsylvania Avenue, N.W. (202)456-1414
Hours: 10 a.m.–noon, Tues.–Sat. In summer, pick up tickets at booth on Ellipse after 8 a.m. The rest of the year, go to East Visitor entrance on East Executive Ave. between Treasury Building and White House. Private tours (8 a.m.–9 a.m.) can be arranged through your congressman or senator but request well in advance of desired date of visit. Closed some holidays and for special functions. Admission free.

Wolf Trap Farm Park for the Performing Arts
Vienna, Va.
(703)225-1860 box office; 255-1900 information
Hours: Dawn to dusk. Call information for performance times.
Admission free for park. Tickets required for performances.

Kidding Around with John Muir Publications

We are making the world more accessible for young travelers. In your hand you have one of several John Muir Publications guides written and designed especially for kids. We will be *Kidding Around* other cities also. Send us your thoughts, corrections, and suggestions. We also publish other young readers titles as well as adult books about travel and other subjects. Let us know if you would like one of our catalogs. All the titles below are 64 pages and $9.95, except for *Kidding Around the National Parks of the Southwest* and *Kidding Around Spain*, which are 108 pages and $12.95 each.

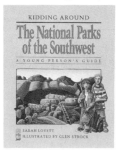

TITLES NOW
AVAILABLE IN THE
SERIES
Kidding Around Atlanta
Kidding Around Boston
Kidding Around Chicago
Kidding Around the Hawaiian
   Islands
Kidding Around London
Kidding Around Los Angeles
Kidding Around the National
   Parks of the Southwest
Kidding Around New York City
Kidding Around Paris
Kidding Around Philadelphia
Kidding Around San Diego
Kidding Around San Francisco
Kidding Around Santa Fe
Kidding Around Seattle
Kidding Around Spain
Kidding Around Washington, D.C.

Ordering Information
Your books will be sent to you via UPS (for U.S. destinations). UPS will not deliver to a P.O. Box; please give us a street address. Include $3.25 for the first item ordered and $.50 for each additional item to cover shipping and handling costs. For airmail within the U.S., enclose $4.00. All foreign orders will be shipped surface rate; please enclose $3.00 for the first item and $1.00 for each additional item. Please inquire about foreign airmail rates.

Method of Payment
Your order may be paid by check, money order, or credit card. We cannot be responsible for cash sent through the mail. All payments must be made in U.S. dollars drawn on a U.S. bank. Canadian postal money orders in U.S. dollars are acceptable. For VISA, MasterCard, or American Express orders, include your card number, expiration date, and your signature, or call (800) 888-7504. Books ordered on American Express cards can be shipped only to the billing address of the cardholder. Sorry, no C.O.D.'s. Residents of sunny New Mexico, add 5.875% tax to the total.

Address all orders and inquiries to:
   John Muir Publications
   P.O. Box 613
   Santa Fe, NM 87504
   (505) 982-4078
   (800) 888-7504